The Ghostly Tales of North Central Texas

Published by Arcadia Children's Books
A Division of Arcadia Publishing, Inc.
Charleston, SC
www.arcadiapublishing.com

Copyright © 2025 by Teresa Nordheim
All rights reserved

Spooky America is a trademark of Arcadia Publishing, Inc.

First published 2025
Manufactured in the United States

Designed by Jessica Nevins
Images used courtesy of Shutterstock.com.

ISBN: 9781467197892
Library of Congress Control Number: 2024950550

Notice: The information in this book is true and complete to the best of our knowledge. It is offered without guarantee on the part of the author or Arcadia Publishing. The author and Arcadia Publishing disclaim all liability in connection with the use of this book.

All rights reserved. No part of this book may be reproduced or transmitted in any form whatsoever without prior written permission from the publisher except in the case of brief quotations embodied in critical articles and reviews.

Spooky America

THE GHOSTLY TALES OF NORTH CENTRAL TEXAS

TERESA NORDHEIM

Adapted from *Haunted North Central Texas* by Teresa Nordheim

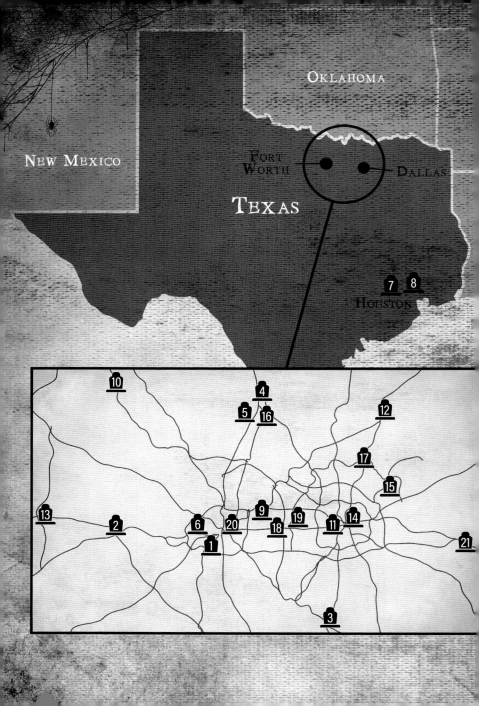

Table of Contents & Map Key

Welcome to Spooky North Central Texas!......... 3

Chapter 1. The First Spooky Story 7

Chapter 2. Haunted Mansions 13
- 1 Thistle Hill Mansion
- 2 Baker Mansion

3 Chapter 3. Catfish with a Side of Ghosts 27

Chapter 4. School Spirits........................ 35
- 4 Texas Woman's University
- 5 University of North Texas

Chapter 5. Lights! Camera! Yikes! 45
- 6 W. E. Scott Theatre
- 7 Former Belaire Theater
- 8 The Majestic

Chapter 6. H$_2$O No! 55
- 9 Screaming Bridge
- 10 Green Elm Cemetery Bridge

Chapter 7. Behind Bars Boos 63
- 11 Old Red Museum of Dallas
- 12 Old Collin County Prison

Chapter 8. Towers of Terror 73
- 13 The Baker Hotel
- 14 The Adolphus

Chapter 9. Graveyard Ghosts 85
- 15 Mills Cemetery
- 16 IOOF Cemetery

Chapter 10. Spooky Attractions 95
- 17 Dark Hour Haunted House
- 18 Six Flags over Texas
- 19 Reindeer Manor
- 20 Cutting Edge Haunted House
- 21 Thrillvania Haunted House

A Ghostly Goodbye 105

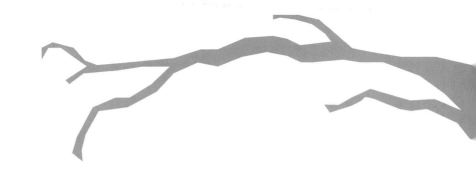

Welcome to Spooky North Central Texas!

Texas is so big that it could hold every ghost from every haunted house in America. That means over a million ghosts could call it home! Each one would have a private, old mansion and a creepy cemetery. That is way too many ghosts for a single book!

The Lone Star State has an incredible history, influenced by the many people who once lived here. The first to call the area home were the Indigenous people called Caddo. The Caddo discovered ample water and flat land ideal for farming, fishing, and hunting. They lived here happily for over three hundred years.

Later, Spanish missions dotted the landscape. French settlers tried to rule but fled due to misfortunes. British traders established bustling outposts. Mexicans wanted to expand their territory. Each country left its mark on Texas, and the state underwent rapid transformation in the nineteenth century. The Republic of Texas emerged on March 2, 1836,

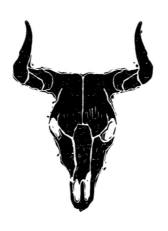

breaking free from Mexican rule. On December 29, 1845, Texas joined the United States as its 28th state, marking a new chapter in its history.

With so much history, it's no wonder Texas is a ghost hunter's delight. There are countless opportunities to encounter ghosts. First, we must decide where to begin our journey. How about the vibrant city of Dallas? If we start in Dallas, we could stretch to the left, the right, and the top of the state. I can introduce you to a few ghosts in north central Texas. Come along!

The First Spooky Story

Caddo traditions were vital in shaping Texas's future cultures. If you have ever said the word Texas, you have spoken a Caddoan word. Upon arrival, the Spanish explorers heard the Caddo say "Taysha," which means friends or allies. The Caddo valued peace and wanted to be friends with the explorers. The Spanish explorers had no idea how to spell the word but wanted to honor their new friends. They began calling the area Tejas or Teyas. Years later, the spelling changed to Texas.

With such a long history, it's no wonder that the Caddo have a rich tradition of storytelling. This tradition offered entertainment and preserved history and culture. It also provided us with legends that still resonate today. A Caddo elder likely told the first spooky story in north central Texas. One such legend is that of the Great Spirit and the dreadful dragon.

On the first day of spring, the Great Spirit slumbered. His favorite resting place was deep in the forest and under a waterfall. This spot held a colorful mix of flowers and lush trees. The birds often sang him a lullaby, and friendly animals slept nearby. It was peaceful and quiet.

As he slept, a dragon with shining scales attacked the nearby village. It ate all the food, leaving the villagers hungry. Then, the dragon drank the lake water and knocked over the water tower, leaving the villagers with no water to drink. The dragon then began to spread diseases and made the villagers sick. The villagers begged, "Please, Great Spirit, help us stop the dragon."

The Great Spirit heard their cries for help. He raced to the village and met the dragon face-to-face. Try as he might, the dragon was no match for the Great Spirit. In the blink of an eye, the Great Spirit buried the dragon deep in the tall mountains.

As the villagers emerged from their hiding spots, the devastation brought by the dragon greeted them. Tears rolled down their faces as they began to sort through the mess. They should have been angry, but they weren't.

The smallest villager smiled and said, "Thank you, Great Spirit."

Filled with joy, the Great Spirit spoke: "When you feel the Earth shake. When you see the lava flow from the volcano, remember that my power protects you."

The Great Spirit made fresh, clean water flow from the Earth and filled the lake. The village, which the dragon wiped out, began to fill with life. Vegetables grew in the rich, brown soil. Trees sprouted delicious fruit, and fish swam in the lake.

The smallest villager was too sick to enjoy the fresh food and water. In his kindness, the Great Spirit knew what he needed to do.

"Follow me," he said to the villagers as he scooped up the smallest villager in his arms. He guided them all to his secret resting place. "This place holds healing waters to keep you strong and healthy." From that day forward, the villagers lived free from trouble and worry.

As you read this book, see if you can find this place in Texas by what reminds you of the Caddo tale. What would you do if you stumbled upon a hidden spring in Texas? And where do you think that dragon lies, hidden under the mountains? Let's continue our adventure to search for magical water, friendly ghosts, and spooky stories.

Haunted Mansions

Imagine this: a cold, dark Texas night. Lightning knocks out the power, plunging you into a world of darkness. The wind howls outside. The thunderstorm grows closer. You count the seconds between each boom and flash. It's like a scene from a scary movie, and you are the main character, alone in the dark.

Out of nowhere, the sound of heavy footsteps on the stairs breaks the silence. The floor creaks, and the footsteps grow louder and louder. Each step increases the suspense. You crawl under the blankets for protection, and your heart pounds in your chest. The bedroom door squeaks as it slowly opens. A gust of wind blows the blankets off your head. A mix of fear and defiance surges through you as you shout, "Who's there?" It's an attempt to hide your trembling heart. You turn on the lamp, but the room is empty except for you and your shadow.

    This is an example of a classic haunted house. Ghosts don't discriminate. They appear at will, haunting wherever they please. They might choose a grand estate, a small cave, or your bedroom. In north central Texas, ghosts often appear in the area's many historical mansions, each with a tantalizing tale that adds a twist to the classic haunted house story. Here are just a few of them.

The Haunting of Thistle Hill

The past can be haunting, particularly at Thistle Hill in southwest Fort Worth. It was built by William "Tom" Waggoner, a wealthy rancher and oil tycoon. He had three children—two sons and a daughter—to share his riches. He favored his daughter, Electra, who seemed always to be in trouble. She was a magnet for mischief. Mr. Waggoner knew he needed to keep a watchful eye on her.

When Electra was young, Mr. Waggoner feared she would move far away when she grew up. He commissioned a magnificent mansion on his land for her as a wedding present, knowing that if she accepted his generous gift, he could keep her close. He didn't cut any corners. Beautiful, lush gardens covered the grounds. Inside, expensive furniture filled each room. In 1904, Electra and her new husband moved into "Thistle Hill." The mansion, a symbol of her father's love and wealth, was heartwarming to Electra.

In the early 1900s, the oil business boomed, and Fort Worth's elite enjoyed extravagant lives. In her unique way, Electra reflected the times by embracing life to the fullest. She didn't lose sleep over what others thought. Electra earned the title of "Princess of the Panhandle." She was the first customer to run up a bill for $20,000 at the Neiman Marcus department store. She had fresh flowers delivered to her home every day. She also had the latest fashions sent to her from Paris and New York. She insisted on being the first to try new outfits but never wore the same one twice. She celebrated in style with her friends. She traveled the world and collected trinkets along the way. After one trip, she even came back with a tattoo! It was unusual for a woman of her background to get a tattoo, especially in the early 1900s.

Electra's wild and daring lifestyle took a toll on her body. She passed away at the young age of forty-three, leaving behind a legacy of intrigue. How would Electra spend her afterlife? Her father, as well as others, believed she would stay at Thistle Hill.

In the 1970s, new homeowners were restoring the old mansion, which had become worn from age. The remodeling disturbed the ghosts, and the spooky sightings began. Guests reported seeing a woman in a white lace gown floating through the home. With the vision came a gentle breeze. The ghostly woman appeared at the top of the grand staircase, where Electra frequently stood. The transparent figure sent shivers down spines. It looked like Electra Waggoner.

Aside from the female spirit at Thistle Hill,

guests see a man in shorts and a polo shirt. He looks ready to play a game of tennis. His fancy mustache curls up on both ends, giving him a unique look. Sometimes, people see him in dress pants, a gray sweater, and fancy shoes. Was he a former resident or a party guest? No one knows.

At Thistle Hill, unexplained footsteps, voices, and music echo throughout the property. Items in the home often move without anyone around, intriguing ghost hunters. In 1997, a team of ghost hunters spent the night in the old mansion. They focused their investigation on the ballroom, which held the most ghost stories. Electra threw all her parties there. According to stories, phantom music still plays over whispers of invisible guests. In the center of the room, the investigator located a ninety-year-old rocking chair. They watched as it began to move on its own. A sheet meant to cover the chair and protect it from dust fell to the floor silently. The sight sent chills down the spines of the brave investigators. Their hearts pounded in anticipation. They put the sheet back on the chair. They then left to investigate other areas in the mansion. When they returned, the sheet was back on the ground! The recorded video proved no one had entered the room. The team had no explanation for this confusing finding. Was Electra getting ready for another party?

The Curse of Baker Mansion

In 1890, John Baker took a gamble by opening a dry goods store in Weatherford, Texas, with his friend George Poston. The shop stocked essential goods for its customers, who could buy anything from fabric to flour. Mr. Baker's hard work paid off within four years of opening. The men became wealthy. Mr. Baker set out to craft a splendid Victorian home for his family. It seemed like his dreams were coming true. However, a series of disasters struck the Baker family that same year, souring their streak of good luck.

The first tragedy was with Mr. Baker's twelve-year-old daughter, Ethel, who became sick. Her doctors didn't know what was wrong. She continued to grow sicker and began having extreme pain all over her body. She died before her thirteenth birthday. Five years later, on a calm Easter morning, Mr. Baker passed away. He never got to see his grand mansion finished.

In 1904, almost fourteen years after construction had begun, Alice Baker and her three adult children, Charles, Henry, and Mary, moved into the mansion. A few months after moving in, Charles left for a business trip. He planned to travel from Texas to California, then to Washington. Somewhere between California and Washington, Charles disappeared. His family feared the worst. They hired a private detective to search for Charles and offered a $5,000 reward. Charles had vanished without a trace. As the case grew cold, the search stopped. His family declared him dead. He would never return to Texas, at least not in human form. The family felt they were cursed.

In 1924, Henry left for a business trip to Chicago, Illinois. He went to the hospital when his appendix ruptured. It was too late for treatment, and he passed away there. Alice and Mary remained in the home until 1942, when Alice died in the mansion. As the last Baker, Mary decided to sell the mansion. She hoped the sale would end the Baker curse.

George Fant purchased the home with his second wife, Elena. They moved in shortly after Mrs. Baker's death. They ignored the rumors of ghosts and settled in to enjoy their new home. Life was good, and they had everything they had ever wanted. But it soon became clear that the curse hadn't ended when the house sold.

In Mr. Fant's previous marriage, he had two children, a son and a daughter. Suddenly, Marian, his seven-year-old daughter, died without warning. His son, Knox, enlisted in the Air Corps and left for training. Mr. and Mrs. Fant continued to live alone in the big house. Then, Mr. Fant received a call from the Air Corps. His son Knox was training on a plane and preparing to fight in the war. His plane crashed, and Knox didn't survive his injuries.

Mrs. Fant's thirteen-year-old niece, Betty, began to visit. The Fants enjoyed having a teenager in the house. In 1962, Mr. Fant passed away in the mansion. It was then that Betty began to detect something unusual about the house. She feared people would tease her if they heard about her experiences, so she refused to tell anyone.

On one visit, Betty heard whispers and footsteps in the empty hallway. Her aunt was asleep, and all the staff had left for the day. Who could it be? Was she going crazy? Betty couldn't keep these experiences to herself. She began writing in a journal every night. Strange things didn't happen every time she visited her aunt, but they happened often.

One night, Betty heard footsteps as she closed her journal. The thumping grew louder until it reached the entrance of her bedroom. The door swung open, and a shadow approached the bed. Betty couldn't believe her eyes. There, at the foot of her bed, stood a tall, dark, shadowy figure. She let out a bloodcurdling scream. By the time her aunt reached her room, the shadow was gone.

One time, Betty ventured into town. "Sometimes I worry about your aunt," the salesclerk said as she rang up Betty's items. "There are stories about that house."

Unfazed, Betty grew curious. "I'd love to hear one."

The clerk leaned over the counter and whispered, "You heard about Charles Baker's disappearance?"

Betty nodded.

"You know that the previous owner of the house, Mrs. Baker, loved to entertain. One night, during one of her parties, guests heard a strange noise. Suddenly, the door on the armoire in the corner flew open. A starched shirt collar rolled out. It rolled past the party guests and stopped at the glass doors." The clerk paused to take a deep breath. "You'll never guess whose armoire and shirt collar it was."

"Charles Baker?" Betty asked.

"It's like Charles was there that night with them," the clerk said.

"He still is," Betty said as she grabbed her bag. Even though it was disturbing, she felt better knowing she wasn't alone in believing in ghosts at the mansion.

In the spring of 1976, Betty's innocent visits turned unpleasant. One time, she was alone. Her husband was traveling for business, and her aunt had moved into a smaller home next door. The night brought a predictable Texas thunderstorm. Fierce winds cut the power; the only light came from lightning bolts. Betty heard a loud pounding. She grabbed a flashlight and made her way downstairs. The ominous noise stopped as she neared the basement door. Then, the door handle shook, and the entire door rattled. For the first time, Betty felt a sense of dread. She ran out of the house, and from that night forward, she believed in the curse.

Catfish with a Side of Ghosts

In 1895, farmer Ezekiel Anderson built a charming Victorian mansion. Years later, the home underwent renovation and opened as a restaurant. The Catfish Plantation is closed now, but in its time, it served authentic Southern cooking. The food was excellent and came with a free side of ghosts.

After the restaurant opened, it took the staff a short time to notice something unusual about their work. They often heard voices when the room was empty and objects moved on their own. They felt they were never alone, even when they were alone.

Several grew curious and wanted answers. They decided to investigate the building's history and learned about deaths and tragedies. On a cold night, a group of brave staff members gathered around a table. They placed a white candle in the center. The makeshift séance was the first proof of ghosts.

They gathered hands as one member asked, "Is anyone here with us tonight?"

To their surprise, they heard a knock on the wall. Then, the dishes in the cupboards began to rattle. The candle erupted into a brilliant, burning ray of light. Everyone sat in silence.

The kitchen doors flew open. A young woman dressed in a flowing white gown entered the room. She hovered a few inches above the floor. The people at the table noticed goosebumps on their arms. The woman circled the table, leaving behind the scent of fresh roses. Before anyone could speak, she disappeared.

Even as the years passed, this female ghost remained. She was said to enter the dining room and lightly touch customers as they ate. Guests said she was gentle, pleasant, and smelled like roses. A lucky few had seen her float into the room in her flowing gown.

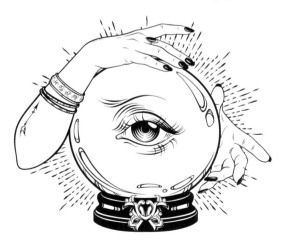

Could she have been Elizabeth Anderson, Ezekiel's daughter? Records report Elizabeth married at a young age and died soon after the wedding. Legend says Elizabeth's jealous ex-boyfriend crashed the wedding. He then took her life. If he couldn't have her, the story goes, no one could.

Another ghost at the restaurant could have been Carrie Mooney. She lived in the Victorian home during the 1950s and stayed there until the 1980s. Carrie loved cooking and entertaining guests. She disliked alcohol so much that she refused to drink or serve it.

Staff and guests began to call this spirit Caroline. To the staff, she could be a mischievous troublemaker. She liked a good prank, and her playful mischief made dining interesting. But if a guest ordered alcohol, things could get tricky.

Wine was on the menu at the Catfish Plantation. When Caroline was around, staff found broken glasses on the floor at night. It happened so often that the closing staff had to lock up the glasses at night.

One morning, the owner entered the building to the smell of freshly brewed coffee. Although it smelled great, it was surprising. It was early, and the only staff member had arrived much later.

"Hello?" she called out. "Is anybody here?" The only response was the quiet hum of the refrigerator.

After she finished her tasks, she entered the dining room. In the center of the floor sat a large teapot and several coffee cups. They weren't there when she first came to the restaurant, and she was still alone. Caroline must have wanted to entertain her guest.

There was one third and final ghost that appeared. The staff named the ghost Will, and some believed he was a former owner of the home. People driving by the restaurant saw a man sitting on the wooden front porch. He was wearing overalls and a cowboy hat. He didn't do much of anything. Despite his good

behavior, people still called the police. As officers arrived, they spotted the old man, but by the time they exited their cars, he was gone.

Ghosts may not have been on the menu, but they still served an *excellent* haunt at this local restaurant.

School Spirits

In school, teachers teach, and students learn—that's the basic idea. But in some schools, there's more to it. Have you ever gotten a chill walking down an empty school hallway? Or heard whispers when no one was around? Your school may have a ghost or two lurking in the shadows.

From the outside, a school building might seem dull, especially during the day. Ghosts do haunt schools, but they're often shy. Ghosts aren't social and might fear the living. They prefer dark, quiet spots like attics and basements.

When the lights go out and the students head home, that's when the real haunting begins. When did school ghost stories start? Chances are that an older student tried to scare a younger one with a spooky story. Then that student told another, and so on. Before long, a legend was born. Students spread rumors fast in schools. Even the fake stories can seem real.

An old, musty campus is the perfect setting for a chilling story, which is why there are so many ghost stories at universities. Here are a couple of stories from north central Texas colleges.

The Forever Bride

Texas Woman's University (TWU) opened in 1901. Its goals were to educate women and prepare them for jobs. Workers constructed the first building in 1903, and a few months later, the first campus ghost story began.

At midnight, music played throughout what is now called Old Main. The building was dark—flipping a light switch to illuminate a room wasn't an option in these early years. Instead, a student struck a match to light a gas lantern, casting a glow across the empty rooms. The students saw desks, chairs, books, and a piano in the far back corner. But no one was playing the piano or running out of the building. Months later, a student confessed to playing a prank. Even though a prankster started this haunted story, there are other ghost tales at TWU.

In addition to the eerie piano, another

tale surrounds Old Main. Another ghost here is said to be that of a teacher who was the subject of cruel mockery and who took his own life. If the school caused his pain, why would the professor stick around? The professor's presence may have two purposes. He protects students and scares away bullies.

One of the most intriguing buildings at TWU is the Little Chapel in the Woods. It was built in 1939, with students playing a significant role in the design. They made the stained glass, art, floors, and lights. Over the years, many couples have said their wedding vows at the chapel. But there's also a tragic story associated with it. A groom decided he didn't want to marry his bride. He never came to the chapel. Consumed by despair, the bride leaped from above. Her fatal plunge from the chapel's heights ended a life too soon. She's now known as the "Forever Bride."

"I have looked into this. There is no death record of a bride," said Britney Jasper, who works at the Little Chapel in the Woods. All the same, "People do feel a strange energy in the chapel," she continued. "Candles go out on their own. Footsteps echo on the empty stairs."

Guinn Hall, named for Dr. John Guinn, is visible almost everywhere in Denton. It is twenty-four stories tall and holds a haunting tale. A young woman plummeted to her death in the year 2000. Reports say the student fell from the ninth floor, but it's unclear if she jumped or someone pushed her off the balcony. Soon after, the college closed access to all balconies. The shock left a lasting mark on the campus. There are reports of footsteps and voices in the building. It might be the student who fell from the ninth floor, however, a dark, shadowy figure also roams the hall. Students believe this figure is Dr. John Guinn. He isn't a troublemaker, but he frightens those who see him floating around.

Prescription for Haunting

The nearby University of North Texas (UNT) has its stories, too. This humble college for teachers opened on September 16, 1890. Joshua Chilton founded the new school in a rental space above a hardware store. It started small, but today, the college has over 50,000 students. As the college grew, so did the stories and legends.

In the early 2000s, an albino squirrel began to appear on campus. Albinism is a genetic condition that causes little or no color in the skin, hair, and eyes. Albino squirrels are so rare that only five places in the United States have them. Texas is not one of those areas.

Students named the squirrel Lucky, and locating the unusual creature became a game.

Campus residents believed that seeing Lucky on exam day meant a good grade. It wasn't easy to find him, but it could make a difference. Some students walked all over campus, hoping to spot the good luck charm.

At least two white squirrels have died at UNT, both named Lucky. One met his fate against a car's tires, and an eagle carried away the other, so neither was very lucky! The science building displays the first Lucky. Experts preserved his body to keep their good luck charm. This is now the only hope of seeing Lucky's body, but some said his spirit lingered. When COVID-19 stopped in-person classes, Lucky's spirit was said to have disappeared.

Animal ghosts aren't the only spirits at UNT. The health and wellness center also hosts a few human ghosts. The first clinic became old and full of cracks and dust. It also creeped people out. Something always felt odd about the building.

One of the doctors shared his chilling experience. "One night, I had to go in and do some charting. I brought my wife with me because I didn't like to be alone in that building," he began his story. "It was old and downright creepy at night." The doctor shook his head as he remembered his experience. He continued, "I asked my wife to run to the car and grab some files from the back seat."

"I nodded," his wife said. "Then I ventured down the empty hall. I went down the stairs toward the front door. It was dark outside, so I moved fast to retrieve the files."

"It wasn't simply the dark," her husband joked.

"No," she agreed. "When I returned to the

building, I saw a dark shadow. Figuring it was a student, I told them the clinic wasn't open. They didn't respond. I heard footsteps moving down the hall and up the stairs toward my husband's office."

"When she reached my office, her face was pale," the doctor said. "She told me about the shadow and footsteps. So, I walked through the entire clinic searching. The building was empty."

Moving into the new building didn't erase the ghosts. The haunted history remained. During the move, the staff took medical equipment. They also brought old blocks and pieces of the building as keepsakes. These items can all hold hitchhiking ghosts. Creepy tales lingered in the air. Stories, once stuck in old walls, now move through new corridors.

CHAPTER 5

Lights! Camera! Yikes!

Picture yourself in a dark, empty theater. A single bulb balanced on a mic stand is the only light. A wire cage protects it. The light casts a creepy glow across the wooden stage. It aims to help actors avoid stumbling into the orchestra pit. Theater workers call this a ghost light. It must stay on, even in an empty theater. Right now, it is adding to the fear factor of the empty theater.

Theaters are superstitious locations. Actors often believe specific actions and words can bring good or bad luck. Wishing an actor good luck has the opposite effect. Instead, saying "break a leg" is best before they go on stage. A bad dress rehearsal means the show will succeed. Many theaters leave a seat open for a ghost, appeasing restless spirits. Theaters have superstitions and great energy. They are perfect for ghosts, who linger not to cause trouble but for the lively atmosphere. Haunted theaters rarely have mean spirits, which is a relief. For some actors, the show must go on. For others, it never ends.

Mr. Scott Goes to the Theatre

When William Scott died in 1961, he left the city of Fort Worth three million dollars. Mr. Scott wanted the town to use his donation to develop the cultural district. Some of that money would fund the W.E. Scott Theater, which the city named in his honor. The theater is a perfect example of luxury, beauty, and culture.

The five-hundred-seat theater opened in 1966. The main entrance had a giant mural and a 575-light chandelier. The theater hosted cultural and artistic performances. Mr. Scott's passion for culture keeps his spirit alive in the theater. He devoted so much time and money to a building he would not see in his lifetime. When the theater opened, his portraits hung in the lobby. The music shook the theater walls with vibrations. Mr. Scott's portraits often needed help to stay straight, which did not please him. Instead of complaining, he adjusted the portraits himself.

While Mr. Scott's spirit lingers, another tragic tale unfolds within the theater's walls. A young man and actor, Kenneth Yandal, volunteered at the theater for two years. The manager made him a job offer in the end, which Mr. Yandal was proud to accept. Sadly, however, Mr. Yandal suffered from depression. When his girlfriend left him, he lost his will to live. He took his own life in the prop room on January 7, 1970, but it seems his spirit never moved on. Visitors report seeing Mr. Yandal onstage wearing a brown suit. Footsteps cross the stage and go up and down the stairs. Items fall off shelves, and power tools turn on when no one is around. His appearance surprises visitors in the basement.

Hide-and-Seek at Belaire

It's not true that only old locations have ghosts. The reality is more complex. Belaire Theater is still a relatively new place, but both staff and guests believe ghosts haunt the theater. Some ghosts are friendly, and others are sinister and dark. When a psychic named Cheryl visited the theater, she felt many ghosts. She was able to identify and describe a few of them.

Cheryl first encountered a playful ghost. "There is a young girl here. She is vibrant but innocent." Theater visitors claim to see a young girl walking alone. They try to interact with her, but she disappears in and out of the walls. It appears she wants to play hide-and-seek.

"This man tells me he used to work here," Cheryl began. "I feel sadness, or maybe it's fear. His life ended abruptly, but he comes across as a gentle and kind man. "Perhaps he is the theater employee who died of a heart attack while running the projector."

Cheryl encountered several friendly spirits. Thinking back, she said she should have stopped while she was ahead. She described the final ghost

as a dark force. "I can feel a heavy sensation, as if an intense and severe pressure is holding on to me. When I try to move, it is like I am trying to run, but I am in a swimming pool filled with water." Cheryl decided it was time to leave when she felt hands tightening around her throat.

The Mysteries of Majestic

In 1904, a friend approached Karl Hoblitzelle with an idea. Mr. Hoblitzelle made his money by investing in real estate. The friend recommended that he invest in theaters. The idea was exciting. Not only did he want to open a chain of theaters, but he wanted them to be the best. He wanted luxury items like air conditioning and sound for the films. In 1921, Mr. Hoblitzelle hired a famous architect. If anyone could turn his vision into reality, it was John Eberson. After all, his nickname was "Opera House John." His designs for the Majestic exceeded the plans.

On April 11, 1921, the Majestic Theater opened for business. Mr. Hoblitzelle ran it with immense pride. He oversaw all operations. In 1922, he was the first man in the United States to add air conditioning to a theater. In 1930, he was the first man in the Southwest to add sound to the films. In 1951, he sold his company to United Paramount. Hoblitzelle loved to be in control. So, he kept all management rights to his 165 theaters.

When he died in March 1967, some believed he stayed in the theater. The Majestic, being one of the first luxury theaters, was exciting enough to entice even a ghost. Visitors and staff began to report doors opening and closing on their own. If they turned off a light, it would flicker back on. If they turned a light on, it flickered off. Sometimes, the lights did this when no one was around. Strange smells floated around the theater. Cold gusts of air hurried past guests. There was little doubt the place had at least one ghost.

News journalist Joy Tipping said, "I worked at the theater in my twenties. It was always so cold that I needed a sweater to keep warm." One night, Ms. Tipping left work after dark. Paranoia gripped her and delayed her departure. Did she lock the door? She checked, rechecked, and checked again that the door was locked. But the next day, she found her

office *unlocked*. Impossible! She spoke with security, who verified that no one had entered or left the building. She demanded to see the videotapes. The guard's story was true, but she knew she had locked the door.

Ms. Tipping didn't know that she worked in Mr. Hoblitzelle's old office. It was her office door that he'd once used to enter the theater. He often came late at night to work when it was quiet and everyone else had left.

It seems the Majestic now has more than air conditioning and sound for its films ... it has a phantom owner.

What would *you* do if you were alone in a theater with a ghost?

H₂O No!

One oxygen atom and two hydrogen atoms make water. Water is mysterious and vital. It's the world's most crucial liquid. But water, the life-giver, can also be a ruthless life-*taker*. The human body is around sixty percent water. Yet, humans can die if we inhale even a quarter of a cup of water into our lungs. This truth warns us of water's power and danger. It urges us to respect its force.

Water can boost energy and let ghosts manifest. Most water hauntings are residual, which means they appear like a movie playing over and over. The repeated playback can be visual, auditory, or even scent.

Two haunting tales show the mysteries and dangers of exploring water ghosts.

The Screaming Bridge

In north central Texas, the winter of 1961 proved unbearable. Snow and ice covered the ground in a glistening layer of white crystals. Dallas had its coldest weather ever in January and February.

On February 4, 1961, six teenage girls visited the city to catch a movie. The psychological thriller got their hearts racing. After the movie, they decided they weren't ready to go home. Instead, they decided to check out "Screaming Bridge," a popular spot for local teens. The bridge had a bad reputation due to all the lives lost there over the years. The girls wanted to take a chance that night. They hoped for an adventure they would never forget.

As they neared the bridge, the driver dimmed the headlights. The heavy snow had created a blinding white curtain, making it difficult to see the road. With a surge of fear, the driver pressed the gas pedal with her foot. The car propelled forward and jerked onto the old bridge. If she drove fast and straight, the driver told herself, they would reach the other side of the bridge safely.

What the girls didn't know, however, was that the bridge was damaged. Just a few days earlier, four high school boys had decided it would be funny to pull an epic prank. Using a match and a pile of straw, they'd lit a small fire on one end of the bridge—but the fire had quickly spread and created a gaping hole.

Crews couldn't make quick repairs, so instead, they placed signs to warn drivers to take extra precaution. The signs might have worked well, but vandals stole them.

Just as the girls' car reached the bridge, a man named Bill Young sat in his car on the other side. He flashed his lights and honked his horn. He soon realized the oncoming car hadn't seen his warning as it raced toward him. Mr. Young heard the brakes shriek and then the girls' screams. He froze as the vehicle dove into the thirty-five-foot ditch below. His warning was the only hope the girls had. Sadly, the snowy night concealed his efforts.

The driver of the car and two passengers died on that frosty night in February. The other three passengers suffered significant injuries. Visitors say they sometimes hear screams from beneath the bridge. The screams from the girls now join the screams of others who died at this location.

The Woman on the Bridge

George Francis told his tale to a local reporter in 2002. Listeners sat on the edge of their seats as they heard a real ghost story unfold. Mr. Francis traveled west with three ranchers to buy cattle. It was October 1948, and in the Texas sun, the small car was blistering hot despite the fact that it was fall. The men drove for several hours. Fatigue set in, and they knew they needed to stop the vehicle.

"We had to stop for a nature break," Mr.

Francis said. "We had been driving for hours, and although we were close to home, we decided to pull over."

They stopped at the midpoint of the Green Elm Cemetery Bridge. The weary travelers burst from the vehicle to flex their arms and legs. As the men moved about the bridge, they inhaled the fresh air. It was quiet, and they were alone.

Then, suddenly, a bloodcurdling scream filled the air. It couldn't have come from more than a few feet away, and the men began searching for the source. It sounded like a female who needed help. They located the source about one hundred feet away.

Mr. Francis reported, "We saw this thing. It floated about eighteen to twenty feet above the river. It rushed toward the bridge." As the strange object grew closer, they saw a woman in a long, white dress. She thrashed in the water as if drowning, and the sea began to carry her body away. She screamed and moaned.

They stood in silence, frozen in fear. Should they run, hide, or jump back in the hot car? Should they dive into the water to save a woman?

Then, the shadow rose. It floated over the bridge, over the men, and off toward the cemetery. She vanished. The four men raced to their car and sped away.

They shared a silent pact to keep the encounter a secret. They knew how unbelievable it would sound. Mr. Francis recalled, "A fella doesn't forget that thing. It stays with you always."

The burden lifted from Mr. Francis as he shared his tale. His story drew curious souls to the bridge, hoping for their own stories. Even now, people visit the bridge, hoping to meet a ghost.

CHAPTER 7

Behind Bars Boos

The Wild West refers to a time in U.S. history when people moved west to explore and settle new lands. Towns sprang up fast, often around railroads and mines. These new towns needed a way to enforce laws and protect citizens from outlaws and bandits. The frontier's peacekeepers faced significant challenges. They had to restore order in a chaotic land.

Starting about 1867, cowboys began herding

cattle in the Wild West. They traveled the Chisholm Trail from Texas to Kansas. Cowboys flocked to Fort Worth's stockyards to sell cows for cash. They unwound from long trips here and rested before the next journey. This center of business and friendship became a key stop on the Chisholm Trail.

The problem was that both sides of the law found the area appealing. Along with the cowboys came the outlaws who lived outside or beyond the law.

Texas was a haven for some of North America's most infamous outlaws. Sam Bass robbed trains with his gang. The Wild Bunch, led by Butch Cassidy and the Sundance Kid, caused trouble. They were famous for their bold train robberies and jail escapes. Even in the 1930s, the bank-robbing duo of Bonnie Parker and Clyde Barrow called Texas home. Jails and prisons weren't a luxury in the Wild West. They were a necessity. Today, some of those outlaws from the Wild West's gunslinging past have chosen to stay in the location of their greatest exploits.

Haunted by the Past

The rapid growth of Dallas's population brought mayhem to the city. Officials wanted to restore order through law. This called for the creation of new courthouses and jails.

In 1892, officials built a castle-like

courthouse made of striking red sandstone. The bright color gave the building its nickname, Old Red. The building's history tells the good and bad sides of the justice system. One case left a mark that still haunts Dallas. The city of Dallas hides this secret deep in the archives.

On March 17, 1844, an enslaved woman and mother named Jane set a record. She was the first person listed on a bill of sale in Dallas. For a mere four hundred dollars, John Young purchased Jane.

With no control over her own life, Jane found herself passed from family to family. She became the property of the Elkins family, who loaned her to Andrew Wisdom. Mr. Wisdom lost his wife and needed someone to help care for his two young children. The children loved Jane, and she did her best to provide for their daily needs. But in 1853, Jane stood in the courthouse, charged with the murder of Mr.

Wisdom. Was she guilty? If so, why did she do it? What could make a sweet caregiver turn into a killer?

It was Jane who reported Mr. Wisdom's death. She accused another man of the crime, but no one heard her plea. Trial notes said Mr. Wisdom slept while Jane made her attack. The judge asked, "Did you assault Mr. Wisdom with an axe?"

Jane shocked the room of spectators when she said, "Yes, and I'd do it again." Gasps filled the room as her words sliced through the heavy air, a stark contrast to the silence that followed.

Records later told the story of terror. Mr. Wisdom was an abusive man. Jane tolerated his abuse to protect the children, but the longer she stayed, the weaker she became. In the end, the abuse accusation didn't matter to the court—they believed Jane's actions didn't show self-defense and found her guilty of murder.

Jane became the first woman executed in the state of Texas, and she wouldn't be alone. Others would meet the same fate in Dallas. From 1891 to 1923, sixty-five executions took place at Old Red. Some believe the trapped souls of the executed linger today, still imprisoned around the building, seeking justice or revenge on their executors.

Twilight hides the courthouse. A scary presence lurks within. Towering and shadowy, it glides through the dim halls. The staff whispers of its eerie existence to not frighten visitors, but as dusk settles, workers hurry home. Groans and moans shatter the silence as the past haunts the present, echoes of those sixty-five executions forever etched into the shadows of Old Red. Among them, Jane's spirit still lingers, a silent witness to the horrors of a flawed justice system.

The Man in the Well

Collin County Prison is one of Texas's oldest jails, dating back to 1880. Builders made the walls with rough-cut blocks of fossilized limestone. Some believe this stone is connected to the jail's ghost.

Hardy Mills vanished on September 2, 1921. Witnesses saw him walking down the street, holding his lunch wrapped in a newspaper. Nothing out of the ordinary, he casually strolled past the farm where he lived.

Two weeks later, farmer Will Baxter saw footprints around an old well on his land. The well's lid sat off to the side, and a horrible odor leaked out. He couldn't believe his eyes as he peered down the dark, deep hole. He saw a human body, partly covered in water. A human head floated on the surface. When police retrieved the body, it was in poor condition.

The coroner identified the body as the missing man, Hardy Mills.

Mr. Mills had lived on the farm owned by Ezell Stepp. Police questioned Mr. Stepp and his nephew Arlyle. It didn't take long for Arlyle to tell the police everything they needed to know. He said he saw his uncle hit Mr. Mills in the head with a hoe. He also saw him stab the victim with a knife. Arlyle confessed to helping dump the body in the well, but he denied killing Mr. Mills.

Police held both men at the Collin County Prison. One of them would never leave the prison walls. A small group gathered in the courtroom to hear the verdict. It didn't take long for the judge and jury to sentence Mr. Stepp to death by execution. When asked for a statement, Mr. Stepp replied, "Well, Judge, I'm not guilty of what I am charged with." On November 17, 1922, a crowd gathered again at the jail. This time, to witness the execution of Ezell Stepp.

Mr. Stepp shouted from his jail cell: "You're preparing to hang an innocent man." He made this declaration one final time before the trap sprung. "I'm innocent of the murder of Hardy Mills," Mr. Stepp declared. Seconds later, his lifeless body hung from the noose.

The eerie, abandoned prison has many ghosts of former inmates. On dark, rainy nights, a ghostly figure emerges in the courtyard where Mr. Stepp died. Footsteps echo in empty hallways. Ghosts bound in handcuffs and shackles rattle as they move about. The legend of Mr. Stepp's ghost is strong. Workers in the building installed window coverings to avoid seeing him hanging in the jail yard.

Towers of Terror

Cowboys traveled to the Fort Worth area to sell cows and stayed for entertainment. They needed a safe, comfortable place to sleep, and the hotels and motels usually provided a place for visitors to rest.

But not all travelers stayed at hotels for shelter. Some used the privacy to hide crimes from the Texas Rangers. Hotels and motels are often the sites of tragic deaths. They happened then, and they happen today. Troubled souls linger in the hallways of these tall towers. Ghosts find a way to make the most temporary places a permanent haunt.

Too Many Ghosts to Count

In 1922, the citizens of Mineral Wells found a way to make money. Their mineral-rich waters were credited with curing illnesses. Travelers came to seek the healing water and needed a place to stay. The locals raised money to build a hotel and got hotel tycoon Theodore Baker to run it. The hotel allowed tourists to spend the night, and the city earned money.

For many years, the Baker Hotel and city profited. Eventually, the money slowed down. Fewer people came for the water, and the colossal hotel needed help to fill its rooms. The hotel closed for the last time in 1972, and the giant building stood vacant for decades.

In 2014, however, the citizens of Mineral Wells raised money to save the iconic hotel. Investor Laird Fairchild and his partners helped secure the needed funds. Construction and renovation began in 2019. Well, it seems the buzz of saws and thumps of hammers awoke some sleepy hotel guests! According to locals, there is no doubt that ghosts live at the Baker Hotel. Some experts even suggest that over forty spirits call it home!

But who are these ghosts, and where did they come from? Some likely took their last breaths at the Baker Hotel, while others may have returned to the luxurious retreat to rest. People originally came to the area for its healing water, which meant visitors often arrived sick. Some died before the water had

time to work its magic, but others met different ends.

Theodore Baker invested his time and money in the building during his lifetime. He continued to give until he had no cash remaining, and the hotel closed. As a ghost, he could enjoy the hotel's amenities without spending a dime. His passion continued after death as he roamed the halls. He ensured that new guests felt the hotel's warmth, even in the chill of the afterlife.

Earl, Theodore Baker's nephew, once managed the hotel. People described him as a workaholic who only left his suite for business. He lived in the Presidential Suite and died there in 1967. His suite harbors a curious mystery. As guests enter the room, a tingling anticipation dances in the air. Unseen hands steal trinkets from their pockets. Where do the items go?

Earl Baker's sweetheart hangs around the

hotel, too. She occupies a suite on the seventh floor, the same suite Earl gave her when they were alive. When she leaves her suite, she appears in a long, white gown and glides inches above the carpet. A sweet, lingering scent appears, a ghostly perfume that hints at her presence. She also likes to leave red lipstick on drinking glasses. She continues to do so as if she were still alive and well.

Records say a young boy, about six years old, also once visited the hotel. His parents hoped the water would cure his leukemia, a type of cancer. But sadly, they were too late. Years after his death, a psychic visited the hotel. She believes she talked to the young boy. Staff and visitors have spotted him bouncing a ball in the hallway. They've also seen him with a big, shaggy dog and an older woman watching.

The hotel's most wicked story happened on January 16, 1948. Fifteen-year-old Douglas

Moore stepped into the hotel for his shift as an elevator operator. The elevator awaited, ready for another day of ups and downs. He had arrived early and had time to visit with his friends. "Watch this," Douglas said. He jumped in and out of the service elevator as it moved between floors. His friends laughed and encouraged him to do it again. Douglas kept bouncing back and forth. Everyone enjoyed the show, and laughter filled the room.

On one jump, however, Douglas misjudged the machine's distance and speed. His upper body was in the elevator while his lower body hung outside. His friends shouted and grabbed his legs to pull him back, but it was too late. Douglas's descent ended in a flash. Spectators stood paralyzed, unable to help. Time crawled as rescuers battled the elevator. From the wreckage, they pulled his mangled body—a stark reminder of his terrible end. In time, eerie sightings emerged. People saw the upper part of a young man's body. Sometimes, the lower half was close by. Some say a cold rush of air still greets guests as they enter and exit the elevator.

Each day, as the sun sets at the Baker Hotel, shadows are cast through the windows. The spirits linger, hoping to tell their stories to a new group of visitors.

Don't Take the Elevator

The Adolphus Hotel stands out in downtown Dallas. Paranormal experts say it is one of the country's top ten haunted places. It opened in October 1912, just in time for Halloween haunts.

Tragedy struck just before the opening, when the hotel's elevator claimed its first victim. Charles McIntosh became wedged between a cage and the elevator shaft. Lifted and dragged, he clung to life for a moment. McIntosh fought hard, but his injuries were fatal.

Tragedy struck again on October 20, 1912, two weeks after the grand opening. A waiter named John took the elevator to the third floor. "Good morning," a coworker greeted him. At the same time, he waited for the service elevator to arrive so he could return to the kitchen.

With his back to the elevator doors, he greeted his coworker. The elevator chimed as it arrived on the floor, and the doors opened. As he stepped back to enter the elevator, it kept moving, throwing him off balance. He fell down the elevator shaft and didn't stop until he landed on the basement floor.

Five years later, in 1917, additional elevator workers died in a tragic accident. A crew performed maintenance on a lift in the hotel's new wing. A crew member fell to the basement and crushed his skull and died. Then, a new face appeared at the elevator controls. James Muse, Jr. was sixteen. His day went as planned until he attempted to enter the elevator on the sixth floor. The doors malfunctioned, and Mr. Muse plunged into the open elevator shaft, falling to the basement.

In 1924, Betasar Calvillo worked as a cook at the Adolphus Hotel. He grew irritated as he waited for the slow elevator to deliver his items. He pried open the doors, wanting to know what caused the delay. His head was crushed when he put it inside the open doors.

On March 15, 1971, Ralph Radley Jr. helped a band load its equipment onto the elevator. After several trips, the band noticed an issue. The doors often opened, but the elevator

car did not arrive. "Check that elevator once more," the musicians cautioned Mr. Radley.

When the bell chimed, Mr. Radley checked. "Yes, it's here." He turned to face the band as he stepped into the elevator. However, the elevator car had continued moving, and Mr. Radley fell to his death.

The Adolphus Hotel is beautiful, but the elevators hold a spooky history. So be warned: Unless you're in the mood to meet some ghostly guests, you may want to take the stairs!

Graveyard Ghosts

Here is an interesting question: Are graveyards for the living or the dead?

At one time in the past, they were, in fact, for the living. Before public parks, graveyards hosted family gatherings. Picnickers spread blankets on lush green grass. Flowers adorning the graves functioned as decoration. Sculptures added elegance to the landscape. Loved ones shared meals and visited one another.

Why might a ghost hang out at the graveyard? There are a few good reasons to float around a cemetery. A lost ghost might not know how to find its way home. If it waited long enough, a loved one might visit its grave, and it could follow them home. Other ghosts might enjoy giving visitors a tiny spook now and then, especially on dark, misty nights when the moon is hiding behind the clouds. Some graveyards might even be like ghost neighborhoods, where spirit friends meet up and share stories from their lives and haunting adventures.

Whatever the reason, many ghosts probably want to be near their families, and a graveyard is a place to reunite. So, it's no wonder these areas often hold ghost stories.

The Legend of Mr. Smiley

The mysterious legend of Mills Cemetery is best told in two parts: the legend and the truth.

The Legend

At first glance, the Smiley family grave looks odd. The tombstone has the names of five family members. Based on their ages, the grave holds a father, a mother, and their three children. Their dates of death all read the same: May 9, 1927.

Locals came up with an explanation that sounds like a Hollywood horror movie. Charles Smiley went mad one day and trapped his entire family in the attic. He tied a rope around his wife Belle's neck. Then, he did the same to his three daughters, Lilith, Greta, and Charlena. He then hung them from the rafters in the attic. When he finished, he looked around the room at the lifeless bodies. He began crying hysterically. Unable to live with his actions, he took his own life.

Mr. Smiley, haunted by his past, roams the cemetery at night. His footsteps disturb the leaves, chilling the air. He moans and flickers lights, scaring people toward his grave with a sinister intent. The legend says, "At the stroke of midnight, lie down on the Smiley grave. You will feel someone wrap their arms around your body. You won't be able to move as a force holds you to the ground. This is Mr. Smiley trying to add more bodies to the grave."

The Truth

From May 7 to May 9, 1927, a wave of storms hit Tornado Alley, an area of nine states, including Texas. The storms killed over two hundred people and injured many more. On May 9, 1927, two tornadoes touched down in Texas between three and four o'clock in the morning.

Several victims died after they became trapped in their beds. Initial reports told of twelve deaths in the city of Garland. The final death toll was seventeen. The Smileys suffered the most significant loss. Charles Smiley, a railroad worker, and his wife, Belle, died. Their daughters, Lilith and Charlena, were also killed in the storm. Two Smiley children went to the hospital for treatment. Greta died at the hospital on the same day as her parents and sisters. Five-year-old Dorit managed to survive the tornado. He was the only Smiley to make it through the tornado. Doesn't it make sense, then, that Mr. Smiley isn't trying to force victims into the grave. This loving father might be searching for his lost son, Dorit.

The Angel Wings

The Independent Order of Odd Fellows (IOOF) Cemetery is the final resting place of many founders of Denton, Texas, including Sam Bayless. Sam was the successful businessperson of a profitable landscaping business and a nursery. In 1919, he had a fatal fight with a worker, which ended in his death. Visitors say his spirit now roams the cemetery. They trust him to watch over the grounds and maintain the landscaping.

The IOOF received its first burial in 1860. It was Anna Carroll, the infant daughter of Joseph

and Celia. Visitors here often report hearing a baby crying. Anna might be waiting for her mother to return. However, another baby may haunt the area, too.

John Anderson and his son Charles opened a private bank in Oklahoma. It was one of the most prestigious banks in the area. With his career set, Charles decided it was time to start a family with his wife, Minnie.

On December 16, 1891, Minnie gave birth to a baby girl. The baby died before her first breath. Four days later, Minnie passed away as well. Both Minnie and the baby found their

final resting place at the IOOF. Charles ordered a beautiful tombstone for Minnie. Shaped like an angel, large wings cover the entire backside. It stood tall above the other tombstones. At the foot of the angel lay a tiny grave. The baby girl lay in the watchful eyes of her mother. Charles

had planned well. Minnie could watch over their child, even after death.

Those who have lived in Denton for a long time know the legend of the angel at the IOOF. The angelic statue, carved from stone, mesmerizes. Visitors report seeing the head and arms moving. The angel may be comforting the crying babies, but this isn't easy to prove.

"During my visit, I took photos of the angel," a witness reported. "A month later, I returned and couldn't believe my eyes. Both the head and the arms were in different positions."

Spooky Attractions

In 1835, Madame Tussaud created her first museum in London, featuring wax sculptures of famous people. Visitors could enter the basement at Madame Tussaud's Wax Museum to view "The Chamber of Horrors" for a small extra fee. Wanted posters and old newspaper articles hung on the walls. Displays featured sculptures of notorious criminals. In the exhibit, actors in eerie costumes and makeup jumped out to scare guests. Those brave enough got to experience one of the first haunted houses ever. This attraction brought in thousands of visitors. But one question remained: *Why*? What entices someone to part with money for a scare?

When afraid, the body shifts into "fight or flight" mode. If the brain registers a threat or danger, it responds by creating a defense. The body responds similarly to any real, perceived, or imagined threat. It releases chemicals and creates a surge of excitement. The heart beats faster, pumping blood and oxygen to the muscles. The pupils dilate to let in more light and improve vision. In real-life situations, this helps protect us. However, it's different in a controlled environment. To enjoy fear, we need to know we aren't in danger. Haunted attractions offer fear without risk. There are no real safety concerns unless you trip and fall. Visitors can relax and enjoy the thrilling experience.

Of course, not everyone can travel to London to see the Chamber of Horrors. The good news is, whether you're from north central Texas or just happen to be visiting, you *too* can experience ghostly adventures! From haunted houses to eerie sites, plenty of spooky fun awaits you in this part of the American Southwest. These attractions mix terror with family fun. Remember, fear levels aren't based on age, though some attractions do have age restrictions.

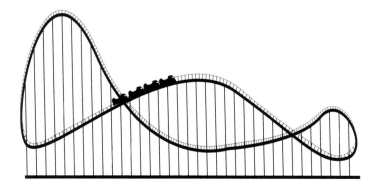

Dark Hour Haunted House in Plano, Texas

This haunted house is genuinely terrifying and suitable for brave souls ages ten and up. The chilling theme unfolds in Coven Manor, held by thirteen witches. Each witch has a unique story and powers. The actors in award-winning costumes bring the sets to life, and the immersive storytelling makes the experience, shall we say, *spooktacularly* realistic.

For those needing a little less terror and a little more spooky fun, they also offer a "Not-So-Scary tour" designed for ages five to twelve. But don't be fooled—the toned-down experience still offers unforgettable frights. The Not-So-Scary tour happens during daylight hours and is fun for the whole family. If witches don't scare you, the eerie ambiance of a creepy carnival might!

Six Flags Over Texas's Fright Fest in Arlington, Texas

The park changes into a spooky wonderland for the Halloween season. It offers a variety of scares, perfect for the whole family. During the day, guests can trick-or-treat and dress up for a costume contest. Characters walk around to meet and greet guests. Six Flags also offers a "no scare" bracelet to signal actors and protect those easily frightened. In the evening, the fear level increases. The park plays on some of the most common fears to build a variety of haunts. A pitch-black maze filled with jump scares awaits those afraid of the dark. A nightmarish circus will put your fear of clowns right to the test. If you haven't yet figured out what scares you the most, don't worry: From eerie aliens to creepy neighbors, Arlington's Six Flags Over Texas's Fright Fest will help you find your fears!

Reindeer Manor Halloween Park in Grand Prairie, Texas

Historical facts make Reindeer Manor—the so-called "oldest haunted house in America"—one of the scarier locations on this list. Imagine an old Texas Manor burned to the ground in 1915, killing the entire family inside. Then, in 1929, just a few years after the house had been rebuilt, the next owner poisoned his wife and took his own life in the barn. Nearly a century later, the Reindeer Manor Halloween Park has been giving visitors frights for generations. With four haunted houses, axe throwing, and live stage shows, there's plenty to see and do. But be careful not to disturb the manor's *real-life* ghosts... they just might decide to follow you home!

Cutting Edge Haunted House in Fort Worth, Texas

According to Guinness World Records, Cutting Edge is the world's largest haunted house. This setting is a two-story, one-hundred-year-old building. Imagine entering an abandoned meatpacking plant. The machines rattle to life. An evil villain has decided to start packaging *humans*. Can you escape before you end up in a box? Thankfully, there is an event called the Haunted House Lite. This version is milder and takes place during the day. There are still jump scares and special effects, but the building has better lighting and focuses on fun. It is best suited for those under the age of twelve. This is an excellent choice for a first haunted house visit. If an abandoned building doesn't scare you, a haunted manor might.

Thrillvania Haunted House Park in Terrell, Texas

This fifty-acre park features many attractions. In 1901, the evil Baron Michael Verdun built a manor. His vampire wife, Lady Cassandra, welcomed visitors. Together, they hosted parties to bring in humans and animals. Verdun wanted to create a human-animal hybrid. Today, it's said their failed attempts still haunt the grounds of the manor in monster form. One a stormy night, a mob attacked the manor, killing the Verduns—could their restless ghosts still roam here, too? For those who are spooked easily, don't worry: the park has designated no-scare zones and a toned-down daytime haunt. But for you, brave ghost hunter, the Thrillvania Haunted House may just be a walk in the park. Witches, clowns, and ghosts hold no terror for you. Deserted structures fail to unnerve your spirit. Even a massive, haunted mansion can't rattle your nerves. Your courage and thirst for adventure know no bounds. *Right?* I guess you'll have to gather your friends, summon your courage, and embark on a haunting adventure to find out!

A Ghostly Goodbye

Our spooky exploration of north central Texas has come to an end...for now. Many of the locations in this book are open to visitors. Are you brave enough to explore a cemetery at night? You could meet Mr. Smiley and his family in Garland. Would you dare to lay on the ground to see if the grave pulls you in? Denton's Independent Order of Odd Fellows Cemetery might be interesting on a quiet night. Listen for babies crying and watch the angel closely to see if her wings flap.

If you want an overnight spooky adventure, try the Adolphus Hotel in Dallas. I recommend that you take the stairs instead of the elevator. The ghosts will welcome you when the iconic Baker Hotel reopens in Mineral Wells. You can book a room and spend the night investigating with a tape recorder and a flashlight. Grab a glass of cool mineral water from the well if you get thirsty during your investigation.

I hope you have enjoyed meeting the many ghosts of north central Texas, and I wish you many happy, haunting adventures.

Teresa Nordheim is thrilled to be diving into the spooky realm of kids' literature! *The Ghostly Tales of North Central Texas* is her first children's book, a companion to her book, *Haunted North Central Texas*. Her passion for writing began in third grade when she entered a writing contest (spoiler alert: she lost). Teresa went on to write over fifty articles for children's magazines, including *Highlights for Children*. With five books under her belt, she has already made a name for herself in the writing world. However, writing for a younger audience is a dream come true.

Teresa works as a nurse during the day and becomes a paranormal detective at night, researching and investigating haunted locations. Although she didn't win, that contest in the third grade sparked a lifelong love for writing. This proves that some things—like stories and spooky spirits—endure forever.

Check out some of the other *Spooky America* titles available now!

Spooky America was adapted from the creeptastic *Haunted America* series for adults. *Haunted America* explores historical haunts in cities and regions across America. Here's more from the original *Haunted North Central Texas* author, Teresa Nordheim: